A PRIMARY SOURCE
LIBRARY OF
AMERICAN CITIZENSHIP ™

The Pledge of Allegiance

Heather Fata

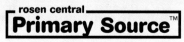

rosen central
Primary Source™
The Rosen Publishing Group, Inc., New York

Published in 2004 by The Rosen Publishing Group, Inc.
29 East 21st Street, New York, NY 10010

Copyright © 2004 by The Rosen Publishing Group, Inc.

First Edition

Library of Congress Cataloging-in-Publication Data

Fata, Heather.
The pledge of allegiance/by Heather Fata.
     p. cm.—(A primary source library of American citizenship)
Summary: Introduces the Pledge of Allegiance, the man who wrote it, how it has changed since it was written, and why some people object to some of its words.
Includes bibliographical references and index.
ISBN 0-8239-4476-X (lib. bdg.)
1. Bellamy, Francis. Pledge of Allegiance to the Flag—History—Juvenile literature. 2. Bellamy, Francis. Pledge of Allegiance to the Flag—Juvenile literature. 3. Flags—United States—Juvenile literature. [1. Pledge of Allegiance. 2. Bellamy, Francis.]
I. Title. II. Series.
JC346.F38 2003
323.6'5'0973—dc22

                                                                                                    2003013943

Manufactured in the United States of America

On the cover: top: photograph by Frances Benjamin Johnston of schoolchildren reciting the pledge; bottom left: photograph of naturalization ceremony on April 25, 2003; background: The Pledge of Allegiance as printed in *The Youth's Companion* magazine on September 8, 1892.

Photo credits: cover (background), pp. 12, 17, 18 © AP/Wide World Images; cover (top right), pp. 7, 9, 13, 14, 15 (top) © Library of Congress, Prints and Photographs Division; cover (bottom left), pp. 26, 27 © Getty Images; pp. 4, 24, 25 © Bettmann/Corbis; p. 5 © Mark Peterson/Corbis/Saba; pp. 6, 15 (bottom), 22 © Corbis; p. 8 © Library of Congress, Prints and Photographs Division, Detroit Publishing Company Collection; p. 11 © Department of Rare Books and Special Collections, University of Rochester Libraries; p. 19 © Library of Congress, Rare Books and Special Collections Division; p. 21 © Hulton/Archive/Getty Images; p. 23 © Library of Congress, Manuscript Division; p. 29 © The National Flag Day Foundation, Inc., Annual National Pause for the Pledge Program, Flag Day, June 14.

Designer: Tahara Hasan; Editor: Nicholas Croce

Contents

 1 The Birth of the Pledge

Children and adults say the Pledge of Allegiance every day. But it is easy to say the words and forget their meaning. The words have a lot of meaning when you think about them. You can understand them better when you learn the history of the pledge. The history of the pledge is very interesting.

Children salute the flag at a school in Chicago on September 9, 1963. Many schools at that time were racially divided. But children of many backgrounds saluted the flag together.

New York City mayor Michael Bloomberg salutes the flag with officials at a fire department ceremony. This ceremony took place on February 28, 2002, in Brooklyn. The pledge has been recited for many years at the beginning of ceremonies like these.

Children are an important part of the Pledge of Allegiance story. The pledge was written for schoolchildren more than 100 years ago. A man named Francis Bellamy wrote the pledge. The pledge first appeared in *The Youth's Companion* magazine in September 1892. It was said by millions of children later that year.

A group of African American children say the pledge in Hampton, Virginia, around 1900. They are raising their hands instead of placing them over their hearts. Raising your hands to salute was the custom at that time.

THE YOUTH'S COMPANION

KIT CARSON ·· HUNTER AND TRAPPER ·· IMPLACABLE FOE OF HOSTILE INDIANS BUT FRIEND AND PROTECTOR OF THOSE THAT WERE PEACEFUL ·· TRAIL MAKER · PATHFINDER · GUIDE ·· INCOMPARABLE SCOUT AND LOYAL AND EFFICIENT SOLDIER ·· THE LAST OF THE OLD FRONTIERS-MEN AND ONE OF THE GREATEST

This is the cover of an issue of *The Youth's Companion* magazine. The magazine was read by young people and even adults. It was a good place to print the Pledge of Allegiance because it was so popular.

Bellamy was a Baptist minister who worked in Boston. He was very interested in helping people make their lives better. He had many new ideas and strong beliefs. But some people did not agree with his beliefs at that time. He was pushed out of the church where he worked.

This is a photograph of the First Baptist Church of Boston around 1901. This is similar to the church Francis Bellamy worked in before he was forced out. After he was forced out he joined *The Youth's Companion* magazine. There, he wrote the Pledge of Allegiance.

This portrait of Francis R. Bellamy was created between 1915 and 1925. Bellamy wrote the Pledge of Allegiance. It continues to be recited today almost as he wrote it in 1892.

2 New Beginnings

Bellamy found a job at *The Youth's Companion* magazine. The owner of the magazine liked Bellamy's ideas. One of Bellamy's jobs was to write a pledge to the flag. Bellamy's boss, James Upham, told him what it should be like. The pledge was to celebrate the 400th anniversary of Columbus's discovery of America.

Salute to the Flag

The Pledge of Allegiance was first called Salute to the Flag. It was later changed to the Pledge of Allegiance.

A pledge of allegiance suggested for the
Columbus Day salute to the Flag — F.B.

I pledge allegiance to my Flag and to the Republic for which it stands — One Nation indivisible — with liberty and justice for all

This is the pledge that Francis Bellamy wrote in 1892. The wording is slightly different than the wording today. The wording of the pledge has been changed several times over the years.

Bellamy was proud of his Pledge of Allegiance. It was published on September 8, 1892. Upham and Bellamy helped set up the Columbus Day program for schoolchildren. The program was to include a reading of the pledge. On October 12, more than 12 million schoolchildren said it.

SALUTE TO THE FLAG, *by the Pupils.*

At a signal from the Principal the pupils, in ordered ranks, hands to the side, face the Flag. Another signal is given; every pupil gives the Flag the military salute—right hand lifted, palm downward, to a line with the forehead and close to it. Standing thus, all repeat together, slowly : "I pledge allegiance to my Flag and the Republic for which it stands: one Nation indivisible, with Liberty and Justice for all." At the words, "to my Flag," the right hand is extended gracefully, palm upward, towards the Flag, and remains in this gesture till the end of the affirmation; whereupon all hands immediately drop to the side. Then, still standing, as the instruments strike a chord, all will sing AMERICA—"My Country, 'tis of Thee."

This copy of the pledge is exactly how it appeared in *The Youth's Companion* magazine when it was first published on September 8, 1892. Since this was the first time it appeared, instructions on how to say the pledge were given.

These children are reciting the pledge. This took place at a public school in Norfolk, Virginia in March, 1941. Notice that they are raising their hands to their foreheads. This was the custom then.

People did not stop saying the pledge after the Columbus Day celebration. Schoolchildren continued to salute the flag and say the pledge. Adults joined them the following year in April 1893. They did this at the National Liberty Pole and Flag Raising Ceremony in Navesink, New Jersey. James Upham was the person who organized the ceremony.

This photograph of a flag-raising ceremony was taken on April 14, 1865. It took place at Fort Sumter in Charleston, South Carolina. This ceremony was like the National Liberty Pole and Flag Raising Ceremony in Navesink, New Jersey.

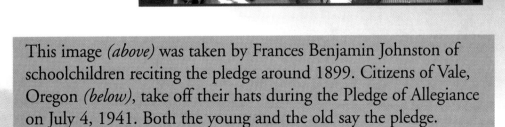

This image *(above)* was taken by Frances Benjamin Johnston of schoolchildren reciting the pledge around 1899. Citizens of Vale, Oregon *(below)*, take off their hats during the Pledge of Allegiance on July 4, 1941. Both the young and the old say the pledge.

3 The Pledge Changes

People soon began to pay more attention to the words. The first change was made on Flag Day in 1923. "My flag" was changed to "the Flag of the United States." Now people would know that the pledge saluted the United States. This change happened during the National Flag Conference in Washington, D.C.

A Change

The word "to" was added to the pledge after it first appeared. It read: "I pledge allegiance to my Flag and [to] the Republic for which it stands."

This photograph is of a woman named Rosie Siller. She is teaching the Pledge of Allegiance to immigrants. They are applying for citizenship. Ms. Siller herself became an American citizen only several years before.

Another change was made the following year in 1924. The words "of America" were added to "United States." It now read: "I pledge allegiance to the flag of the United States of America." This is how it was recorded by Congress in 1942. This is when the United States government officially recognized the Pledge of Allegiance.

Representatives John Stewart and Cameron Brown recite the pledge in Congress on June 27, 2002. The pledge is said at the open of every meeting of Congress.

FLAG DAY

JUNE 14, 1924

PLEDGE TO THE FLAG

" I pledge allegiance to the Flag of the United States and to the Republic for which it stands, One Nation indivisible, with liberty and justice for all."

CEREMONIES ON THE ELLIPSE

AT 10.30 A. M.

This is an invitation to a Flag Day ceremony on June 14, 1924. The invitation has an early version of the pledge written on it. This version was missing the words "of America." Those words were added the day of the ceremony.

The next change to the Pledge of Allegiance came in 1954. Religious groups fought to add the words "under God." The pledge now read "one nation, under God, indivisible, with liberty and justice for all." President Dwight D. Eisenhower approved this change on Flag Day in 1954. This is how the Pledge of Allegiance is known today.

The Bellamy Salute

People raised their right hand chest high until 1942 when saying the pledge. This was called the Bellamy Salute. Now people put their right hand over their heart.

This is a picture of elementary schoolchildren reciting the pledge. This took place in a classroom in Los Angeles in 1924. Notice that the children are raising their hands, as was the custom then, not putting them over their hearts.

4 The Pledge and Religion

In 1940, two Pennsylvania students would not say the pledge in class. Saying the pledge was considered a sin in their religion. They were kicked out of school because of this. The Supreme Court ruled that they had to say the pledge. The court case was called *Minersville School District v. Gobitis.*

This is a photograph of Judge Felix Frankfurter. He was the judge who decided the *Minersville School District v. Gobitis* case. He ruled that children had to say the pledge in school, even if their religion said they could not.

Minersville, Pa.
Nov. 5, 1935

Our School Directors
Dear Sirs

I do not salute the flag be
cause I have promised to do
the will of God. That means
that I must not worship anything
out of harmony with God's law.
In the twentieth chapter of
Exodus it is stated, "Thou shalt
not make unto thee any graven
image, nor bow down to them nor
serve them for I the Lord thy God
am a jealous God visiting the in-
iquity of the fathers upon the children

Billy Gobitis wrote this letter and sent it to the Minersville
School District. It states that he did not want to say the pledge in
school because his religion did not allow him to. This letter led to
the Supreme Court case *Minersville School District v. Gobitis*.

The Supreme Court changed its decision three years later. This case was called *West Virginia Board of Education v. Barnette.* The Court ruled that students could not be forced to say the pledge. And public schools could not punish students for this either. This is still the way things are today.

James, Mary, and Max Morris, shown here, were suspended from school for not saying the pledge. Like Billy Gobitis, their religion said they could not say the pledge in class. They are reading a magazine called *The Watchtower.* The magazine was popular among people who were of the Jehovah's Witness religion.

This photograph from 1941 is of Judge Robert H. Jackson. Jackson ruled that a person could choose not to say the pledge because of his or her religion. This was the Supreme Court case *West Virginia Board of Education v. Barnette* (1943). This ruling went against *Minersville School District v. Gobitis* (1940).

5 The Debate Continues

Some people do not like the words "under God" in the pledge. The Constitution says that the government and the church must be separate. Some people feel that "under God" breaks this rule. In 2002, a court decided that "under God" is unconstitutional. This will now go to the Supreme Court for a final decision.

Michael Newdow, shown here on June 27, 2002, is fighting to take the words "under God" out of the pledge. Mr. Newdow, who does not believe in God, feels that the words are unconstitutional. He believes the words go against the separation of church and state.

A protester stands outside the U.S. Ninth Circuit Court of Appeals on June 28, 2002. This is one day after judges ruled the pledge unconstitutional. One of the judges then put his ruling on hold. A new ruling is expected soon.

Some people believe that government and religion should be separate. Others feel that government and religion should not be separate. The original pledge did not use the word "God." But even our coins have the word "God" on them. This makes the debate even more confusing. Different opinions about the pledge will continue for many years.

Saying the Pledge Together

Pledge Across America is a national school celebration of the Pledge of Allegiance. Students nationwide say the pledge together on September 17 of each year.

"I pledge allegiance to the flag of the United States of America and to the Republic for which it stands, one nation under God, indivisible, with liberty and justice for all."

This chart shows how the Pledge of Allegiance is communicated in sign language. It is very important that all Americans, of all races and abilities, be able to say the pledge.

Timeline

1892 Francis Bellamy writes the Pledge of Allegiance for children.

1893 Adults say the Pledge of Allegiance at the National Liberty Pole and Flag Raising Ceremony.

1923 The Pledge of Allegiance is changed. The words "my flag" are changed to "the Flag of the United States."

1924 The words "of America" are added. The pledge now reads "the Flag of the United States of America."

1940 In *Minersville School District v. Gobitis*, the Supreme Court forces two students to go against their religion and say the pledge in the classroom.

1942 Congress officially recognizes the Pledge of Allegiance.

1943 In *West Virginia Board of Education v. Barnette*, the Supreme Court rules that schoolchildren cannot be forced to recite the pledge in the classroom.

1954 President Dwight D. Eisenhower approves the words "under God" being added to the pledge.

2001 The first Pledge Across America is celebrated.

2002 In *Newdow v. the U.S. Congress*, a court rules that the words "under God" in the pledge are unconstitutional.

2003 The Supreme Court agrees to hear Michael Newdow's case to remove the words "under God" from the pledge.

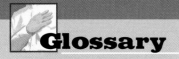

Glossary

allegiance (uh-LEEJ-ents)   Connection to a person, group, or cause.
Congress (CON-gress)   Branch of the United States government that makes laws.
controversy (CON-tro-verse-ee)   A group of different opinions over a topic.
equality (e-QUAL-i-tee)   Equal opportunity and fairness for all.
indivisible (in-de-VIS-uh-bul)   Cannot be separated.
liberty (LIB-er-tee)   Freedom.
pledge (PLEJ)   A promise, or the act of promising.
republic (re-PUB-lic)   A government whose power is in its citizens.
Supreme Court (suh-PREME CORT)   The most powerful court in the
   United States.
unconstitutional (un-con-sti-TOO-shin-al)   Something that opposes the
   Constitution of the United States, or basic laws of a state.

Web Sites

Due to the changing nature of Internet links, the Rosen Publishing Group, Inc.,
has developed an online list of Web sites related to the subject of this book. This
site is updated regularly. Please use this link to access the list:

http://www.rosenlinks.com/pslac/plal

Primary Source Image List

Page 13: Photograph of a color guard saluting the flag at a Columbus Day ceremony in October, 1942 by Marjory Collins. It is currently held at the Library of Congress Prints & Photographs Division in Washington, D.C.

Page 14: Photograph by Roger Smith of radio announcer reading the preamble to the Four Freedoms. This flag-raising ceremony took place in Rockefeller Center in June 1943. The photograph is currently held at the Library of Congress Prints & Photographs Division in Washington, D.C.

Page 15 (top): Photograph of classroom reciting the pledge taken by Frances Benjamin Johnson in 1900. The photograph is currently held at the Library of Congress Prints & Photographs Division in Washington, D.C.

Page 15 (bottom): Photograph of citizens of Vale, Oregon, taking their hats off during the Pledge of Allegiance. It is currently held at the Library of Congress Prints & Photographs Division in Washington, D.C.

Page 17: Photograph of Rosie Siller, a new American citizen, teaching the pledge to a class of immigrants who are applying for citizenship. Photograph taken by Michael Stravano on July 3, 2003.

Page 18: Photograph of Representatives John Stewart and Cameron Brown reciting the pledge in the House of Representatives on June 27, 2002. Photograph by Al Goldis.

Page 19: Actual invitation of the Flag Day ceremony held on June 14, 1924 at 10:30 AM in Washington, D.C. It is currently held at the Library of Congress in Washington, D.C.

Page 21: Photograph taken in 1939 of children reciting the pledge in an elementary school classroom in Los Angeles, California. It is currently housed in the Hulton Archive.

Page 22: Photograph of United States Supreme Court judge Felix Frankfurter, circa 1939.

Page 23: Letter by Billy Gobitis to the Minersville, Pennsylvania, school district from November 5, 1935. It is currently held at the Library of Congress in Washington, D.C.

Page 24: Photograph of James, Mary, and Max Morris taken on November 28, 1940 in Miami, Florida.

Page 25: Photograph of Judge Robert H. Jackson in 1941 in Washington, D.C.

Page 26: Photograph of Michael Newdow on June 27, 2002 in Sacramento, California, by Justin Sullivan.

Page 27: Photograph by Justin Sullivan of Greg Popin protesting outside of the U.S. Ninth Circuit Court of Appeals building in San Francisco, California, on June 28, 2002.

Index

About the Author

Heather Fata resides in Wakefield, Massachusetts. She has a BA in English from Colby College in Waterville, Maine.